50 STATES TO CELEBRATE

Celebrating
MASSACHUSETTS

The text of this book is set in Weidemann.
The display type is set in Bernard Gothic.
The illustrations are drawn with pencil and colored digitally.
The maps are pen, ink, and watercolor.

Photograph of mayflowers on page 32 © 2013 by Brendan Lally as "Mayflowers in the back yard"
    under Creative Commons license 2.0
Photograph of black-capped chickadee on page 32 © 2013 by Brendan Lally as "Black-capped
    Chickadee" under Creative Commons license 2.0
Photograph of right whale and calf on page 32 © 2013 by NOAA/NMFS as "Right whale and
    calf" under Creative Commons license 2.0

Library of Congress Cataloging-in-Publication Data
Bauer, Marion Dane.
Celebrating Massachusetts / Marion Dane Bauer.
p. cm. — (Green light readers level 3) (50 states to celebrate)
ISBN 978-0-544-11972-7 (trade paper)
ISBN 978-0-544-11944-4 (paper over board)
1. Massachusetts—Juvenile literature. I. Title.
F64.3.B38 2014
974.4—dc23
2013006335

Manufactured in China
SCP 10 9 8 7 6 5 4 3 2 1
4500463471

50 STATES TO CELEBRATE

Celebrating
MASSACHUSETTS

Written by **Marion Dane Bauer**
Illustrated by **C. B. Canga**

Green Light Readers
Houghton Mifflin Harcourt
Boston   New York

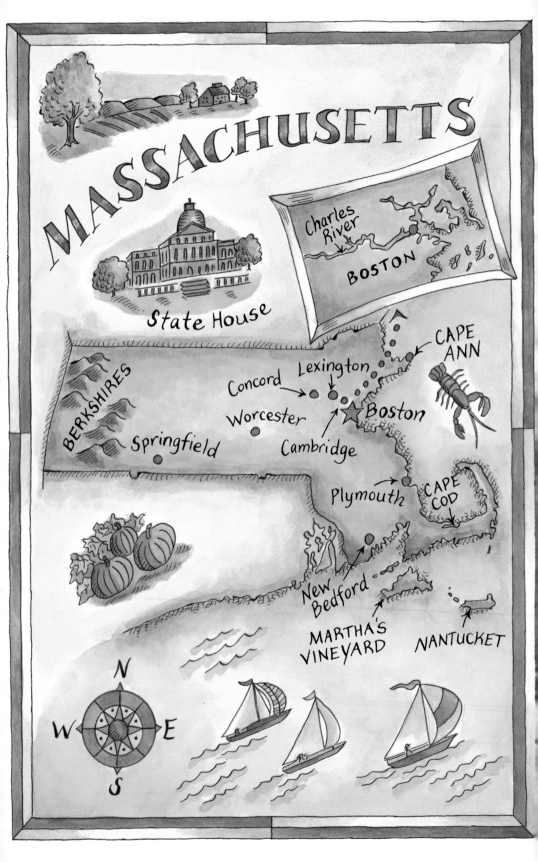

Hi, I'm Mr. Geo.

And here I am visiting Massachusetts.

Its nickname is the Bay State.

Its curving coast borders the Atlantic Ocean.

Massachusetts is one of six states that make up **New England.** The others are Maine, Vermont, New Hampshire, Connecticut, and Rhode Island. 1

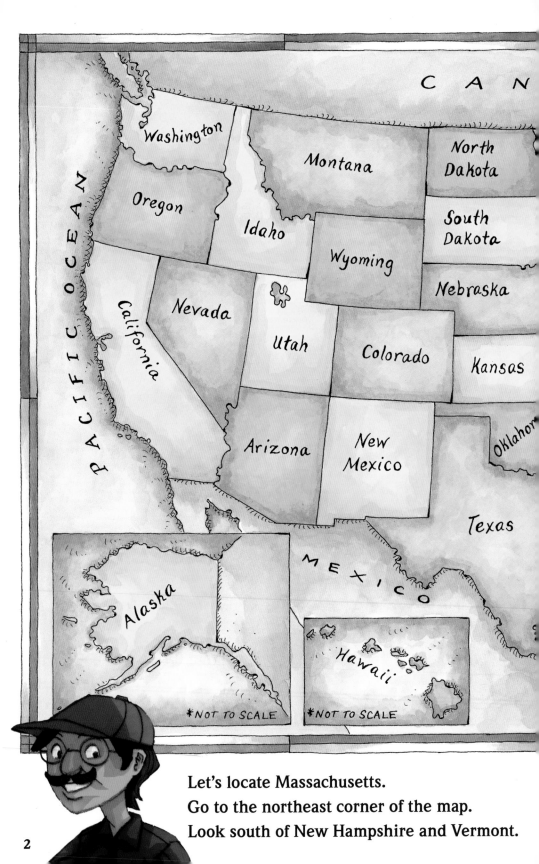

Let's locate Massachusetts.
Go to the northeast corner of the map.
Look south of New Hampshire and Vermont.

2

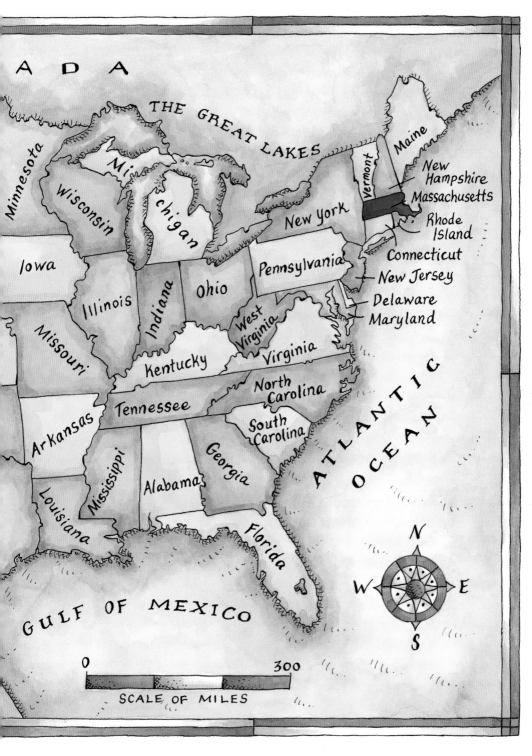

Then look north of Connecticut and
Rhode Island.
Massachusetts is right there in the middle!

Welcome to Boston, the state capital!
You're just in time for one of our nation's
biggest birthday parties.
Yes, it's the Fourth of July, and
I'm camped out by the Charles River.

The Boston Pops Orchestra plays.
The crowd sings along.
Fireworks flare!
Wow! Did you see that one?

Massachusetts was one of the original
13 **colonies** that came together to form
the United States.

Hurrah! I love reliving moments in history.

This Boston Tea Party Ship is a great place to start.

I'm helping **patriots** dump crates of tea

into Boston Harbor.

Together we shout, "No **tax** on tea!"

In 1773, this bold protest against British rule led to

the **American Revolution.**

Faneuil Hall is one of my favorite stops on the trail. Colonists held important meetings here. They shopped here too.

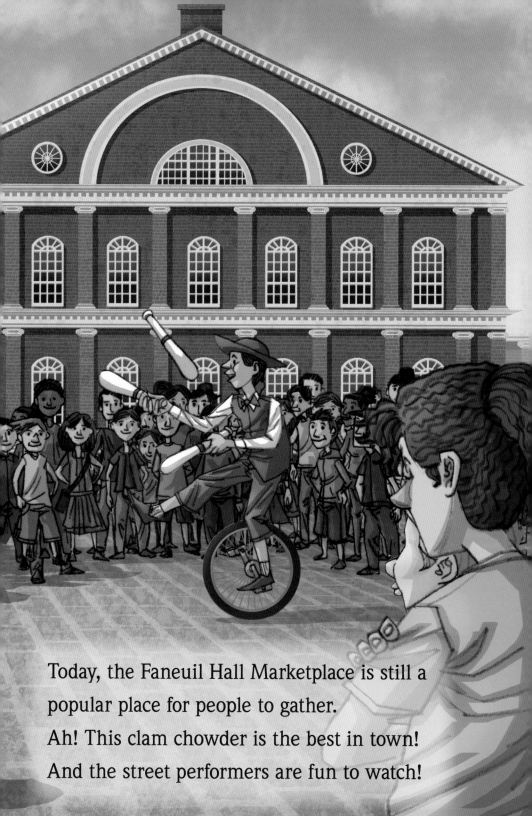

Today, the Faneuil Hall Marketplace is still a
popular place for people to gather.
Ah! This clam chowder is the best in town!
And the street performers are fun to watch!

Now I'm at Paul Revere's house.

Here, we can learn about Revere's famous ride.

His ride began after two lanterns were hung in the steeple of Old North Church.

The lights were a signal that
British soldiers were coming on ships.
Revere then rode into the night to warn
men in the **militia** to be ready to fight.

The American Revolutionary War began
with the Battles of Lexington and Concord
on April 19, 1775.

Summer is baseball time at Fenway Park. *Whack!* That Red Sox slugger just hit another home run!

Fenway Park is the nation's oldest major league ballpark that is still in use. It opened in 1912.

When I visit here in winter, I can watch . . .
the Boston Bruins play hockey,
the Boston Celtics play basketball,
and the New England Patriots play football.
If I come back in the spring, I can run the
Boston Marathon!

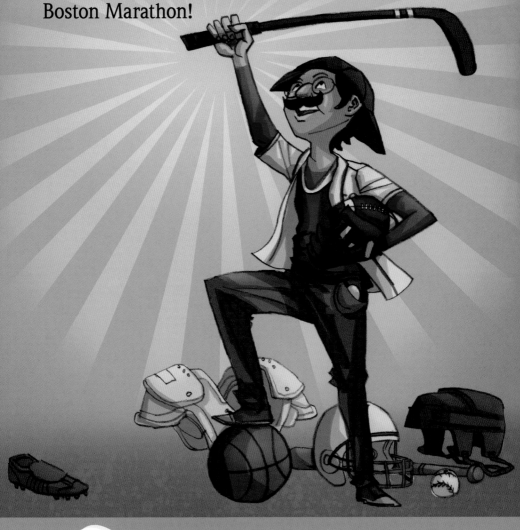

Did you know?

The game of basketball was invented in
Springfield, Massachusetts. The Basketball
Hall of Fame is now located there.

This state is home to more than 100 colleges and universities.

Harvard University, in Cambridge, is the oldest. Nearby, the Massachusetts Institute of Technology is famous for teaching top scientists and engineers.

Many colleges have great rowing teams.
How do they make it look so easy?

Did you know?

Massachusetts was the first state to offer free public schools for children.

The first people in Massachusetts were
Native Americans.
They lived here for thousands of years before
the Pilgrims came from Europe.
Today we can visit a **replica** of the *Mayflower,*
the ship the Pilgrims sailed on.

The Pilgrims landed at Plymouth Rock
in 1620.

At Plimoth Plantation we can see how the
Pilgrims lived.
Right now, I'm pounding corn to make bread.
It takes more muscle than I thought!
Would you like a turn?

The Pilgrims would have starved without help from the **Wampanoag** people.

They showed the Pilgrims how to farm.

When the harvest was ready, the colonists and the Native Americans shared a feast.

That is known as the first Thanksgiving.

At the Wampanoag Homesite at Plimoth Plantation we can visit a Native American home called a **wetu**. We can learn an old tribal game called hubbub. My new friends play much better than I do!

Massachusetts is called the **Bay** State for a reason.
Most of its coast is one enormous bay.
Its harbors are busy transportation centers.
Fishing has always been important here.

And tourists love the rocky coasts and
sandy beaches.
I do too!

Cape Ann lies on the state's northern shore.
That fishing boat just delivered the catch
of the day.
It's lobster for dinner tonight!

And now I am visiting Cape Cod on the state's
southern shore.
I love riding bike trails here and on the islands of
Martha's Vineyard and Nantucket.
We pass cranberry **bogs**, salt marshes,
sand dunes, and lighthouses.
But the very best view is the shining sea itself!

Museums in New Bedford and Nantucket teach
about life on whaling ships traveling from this
state to places around the world 200 years ago. **25**

This state's natural beauty stretches beyond its coast. There are mountains, forests, and **fertile** valleys to explore in central and western Massachusetts. Have you ever seen a pumpkin patch?

Massachusetts farmers grow all sorts of berries, including cranberries, blueberries, strawberries, and raspberries.

Or surprised a whitetail deer in the forest?

Or a fox?

The changing seasons offer many activities.
In the fall I love picking apples, going on
hayrides, and exploring corn mazes.
In the winter, skiing is always a thrill!

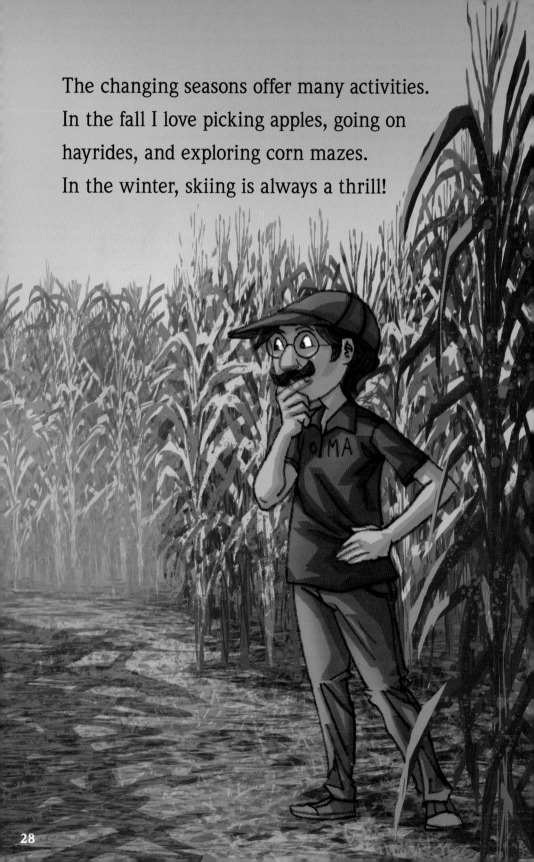

And anytime of year we can experience life
on an old New England farm at Sturbridge Village.
Spring is my favorite time of year, though.
That's when we can count farm babies!

We began our visit in Boston at our
nation's birthday party.
Let's end it here in western Massachusetts.
The setting is perfect for a picnic.
The beautiful Berkshire Mountains surround us.
Sounds from the Tanglewood Music Festival fill
the air.

From east to west, Massachusetts gives us
history and art, learning and natural beauty.
Massachusetts, a small but great state.

Fast Facts
About Massachusetts

Nickname: The Bay State. Also called the Old Colony State in honor of Plymouth Colony.

State motto: *Ense petit placidam sub libertate quietem* (By the sword we seek peace, but peace only under liberty).

State capital: Boston.

Other major cities: Cambridge, Springfield, Worcester, Lowell, New Bedford.

Year of statehood: 1788.

State mammal: The right whale.

State bird: The black-capped chickadee.

State flower: The mayflower.

State flag:

Population: Just over 6.5 million people, according to the 2010 U.S. census.

Presidents from Massachusetts: John Adams, John Quincy Adams, John F. Kennedy, and George H. W. Bush were all born in Massachusetts; Calvin Coolidge lived in Massachusetts most of his life but was born in Vermont.

Dates in Massachusetts History

1600: An estimated 50,000–100,000 Wampanoag people are living in Massachusetts and nearby Rhode Island.

1620: The Pilgrims arrive at Plymouth.

1621: Pilgrims share their first harvest with some Native Americans. This is sometimes referred to as the first Thanksgiving.

1636: Harvard University is founded, the first college in the American colonies.

1773: Colonists rebel against Britain's demand for more taxes by dumping British tea into Boston Harbor.

1775: Battles of Lexington and Concord begin the American Revolution.

1783: Massachusetts outlaws slavery.

1788: Massachusetts becomes the sixth state.

1852: Massachusetts becomes first state to require children to go to school.

1951: The Freedom Trail is established.

1974: The first Fourth of July concert with fireworks, cannon fire, and church bells takes place on the Charles River Esplanade.

1979: The John F. Kennedy Library and Museum opens; it honors our country's 35th president.

2004: The Red Sox win the World Series for the first time since 1918.

2007: Deval Patrick becomes the state's first African American governor.

Activities

1. **LOCATE** the states on Massachusetts's northern border on the map on pages 2 and 3. Then, locate the states on southern border. **SAY** the name of each state you located out loud. What state lies to the west of Massachusetts? SAY its name out loud.

2. **CREATE** the cover for a travel magazine about Massachusetts. Include a picture, a headline, and a caption. On the back, explain why you chose that picture.

3. **SHARE** two facts you learned about Massachusetts with a family member or friend.

4. **PRETEND** you are a tour guide for Massachusetts. A local radio talk show host plans to invite the best tour guide on her radio show as a guest speaker. Answer the following questions about Massachusetts correctly and you will be the tour guide chosen.

   a. **WHAT** did the patriots dump into Boston Harbor in 1773?

   b. **WHO** was the patriot who rode through the night to warn others that the British were coming?

   c. **WHERE** do the Boston Red Sox play baseball?

   d. **WHEN** did the Pilgrims land at Plymouth Rock?

   e. **WHAT** type of home did some Wampanoag live in?

5. **UNJUMBLE** these words that have something to do with Massachusetts. Write your answers on a separate sheet of paper.

   a. **NTERLSAN** (HINT: They were used as a signal at the Old North Church)

   b. **RBNERRYAC** (HINT: a red fruit that grows in a bog)

c. **ELLOCEG** (HINT: a place where people go to learn after high school)

d. **VGINGIHTNKSA** (HINT: a holiday known for feasting)

FOR ANSWERS, SEE PAGE 36.

Glossary

American Revolution: the war that won the 13 American colonies freedom from British rule; it took place from 1775–83. (p. 6)

bay: a body of water that is partly enclosed by land but has a wide opening out to the sea. (p. 22)

bog: an area of wet, spongy ground; cranberries grow in bogs. (p. 25)

colony: a settlement ruled by another country. (p. 5)

fertile: good for plants to grow in. (p. 26)

independence: freedom. (p. 9)

militia: a group that was asked to fight in emergencies. (p. 13)

New England: a term used to describe the six states in the northeast section of the United States; these states include Massachusetts, Connecticut, Rhode Island, Vermont, New Hampshire, and Maine. (p. 1)

patriot: a person who loves, supports, or defends one's country. The leaders and soldiers who organized and participated in the American Revolution were called patriots—they wanted independence from British rule. (p. 6)

replica: an exact copy of something. (p. 18)

tax: money that people or businesses pay to support a government. (p. 6)

Wampanoag: a Native American people who lived in Massachusetts for thousands of years before the arrival of Europeans. Other Native American people who lived in Massachusetts include the Nauset, the Nipmuc, the Pennacook, and the Pocomtuc. (p. 20)

wetu: a dome-shaped Wampanoag home; wetus were made of sticks, grass, and other plants and covered with bark. (p. 21)

Answers to activities on page 34:

1) Vermont and New Hampshire are on the northern border, Connecticut and Rhode Island are on the southern border, and New York is on the western border; 2) drawings will vary; 3) answers will vary; 4a) tea; 4b) Paul Revere; 4c) Fenway Park; 4d) 1620; 4e) wetu; 5a) LANTERNS; 5b) CRANBERRY; 5c) COLLEGE; 5d) THANKSGIVING.